Weather

Kay Robertson

rourkeeducationalmedia.com

www.rourkeeducationalmedia.com

PHOTO CREDITS: Cover: © Chee Ming Wong, : © Vera Kuttelvaserova Stuchelova; page 1: © Skyhobo; page 4: © Josh Judge - WMUR-TV; page 5: © paulprescott72, © mbbirdy, © apomares; page 7: © nicodemos; page 9: © Maksym Darakchi; page 10: © Sabrina Pintus; page 11: © Sergiy Kuzmin, © Mattia D'Antonio; page 12: © Lobsterclaws; page 13: © GhostFly, © NascarNole; page 15: © Wavebreak Media Ltd; page 17: © Gary Whitton; page 20-21: © morkeman; page 22: © CinematicFilm; page 23: © stevegeer, © Malven; page 25: © Matthew Dixon, © DenisTangneyJr; page 27: © Susan Trigg; page 28: © georgemuresan; page 29: © GeorgePeters, © pelicankate; page 31: © Robert Byron; page 32: © Viorika; page 33: © Hans-Joachim Schneider; page 35: © cpurser, © Mikhail Kusayev; page 37: © NOAA; page 38: © NOAA. Parker, CO, © Alexey Stiop; page 41: © NOAA; page 42-43: © coleong; page 44

Edited by: Jill Sherman

Cover design by Nicola Stratford
Interior design by Renee Brady

Library of Congress PCN Data

STEM Guides to Weather / Kay Robertson
    p. cm. -- (STEM Everyday)
Includes index.
ISBN 978-1-62169-849-4 (hardcover)
ISBN 978-1-62169-744-2 (softcover)
ISBN 978-1-62169-952-1 (e-Book)
Library of Congress Control Number: 2013936455

Also Available as:

Rourke Educational Media
Printed in the United States of America,
North Mankato, Minnesota

Rourke
Educational Media

rourkeeducationalmedia.com

customerservice@rourkeeducationalmedia.com • PO Box 643328 Vero Beach, Florida 32964

Table of Contents

Introduction

Have you ever watched the news on television? If so, you may have seen a **meteorologist** give a weather report.

If you listened to your local meteorologists carefully, you probably heard them use numbers to describe amounts of rain or snow, the intensity of an approaching storm, and, of course, the temperature.

And where there are numbers, there is math!

Believe it or not, a meteorologist has to use math every day to determine what all those numbers mean. After you've read this book, you'll understand what they mean, too!

Every day, meteorologists analyze and interpret a vast amount of data such as the rotating updraft in a supercell thunderstorm.

Technology gives meteorologists access to incredible amounts of weather data as they prepare for the news.

Learning About the Atmosphere

A meteorologist is a scientist who studies the atmosphere. The atmosphere is a layer of gases that surrounds a planet.

There are actually several layers to the Earth's atmosphere, but the lowest layer, the one that contains all the gases we depend on to live, is called the **troposphere**.

Like everything to do with weather, the height of the troposphere is always changing.

What meteorologists refer to as weather, including the temperature, rainfall, and storms, is all a thanks to the atmosphere. But the troposphere is where all weather takes place.

STEM in Action?

Generally speaking, the average height of the troposphere around the world is 6 miles. Do you know how many feet that is?

There are 5,280 feet in one mile. To find out how many feet there are in 6 miles, you need to multiply:

5,280 x 6 = 31,680

So you can also say that the troposphere reaches 31,680 feet into the air. That's pretty high!

The highest mountain in the world, Mount Everest, reaches up 29,028 feet (8.85 meters).

Cirrus clouds

Cumulus clouds

Stratus clouds

It is also within the troposphere that you can find clouds. Clouds are actually made of millions of little drops of water. Most of the time, the water in the air is in a **vapor**, or gas, state. Clouds form when there is so much water in the atmosphere that it **condenses**, or changes from vapor to liquid.

There are three basic types of clouds: cirrus, cumulus, and stratus. The cloud type you are probably most familiar with are cumulus clouds. Cumulus clouds are big, puffy clouds. Stratus clouds are layered and flat, and cirrus clouds are thin and wispy.

Along with the three basic types of clouds, there are also clouds that are combinations of different types of clouds. Cirrostratus clouds are a combination of cirrus and stratus clouds.

You already know that clouds can be found in the air, but each type of cloud exists at a different altitude.

Type of Cloud	Altitude
Cirrus	20,000 to 40,000 feet
Cirrostratus	20,000 to 40,000 feet
Cirrocumulus	20,000 to 40,000 feet
Altostratus	6,000 to 20,000 feet
Altocumulus	below 6,000 feet
Stratocumulus	below 6,000 feet
Stratus	below 6,000 feet
Cumulus	below 6,000 feet
Cumulonimbus	cloud mass from below 6,000 feet to over 50,000 feet

STEM in Action

Using this data, can you calculate how much higher up a cirrus cloud is compared with a stratus cloud?

A cirrus cloud can be anywhere between 20,000 and 40,000 feet. Just to keep things simple, use the lower number: 20,000. Meanwhile, a stratus cloud is typically below 6,000 feet. All you have to do to compare these numbers is to subtract the smaller number from the larger one:

20,000 - 6,000 = 14,000

So a cirrus cloud is at least 14,000 feet higher up than a stratus cloud!

Because they are big and puffy, the clouds pictured here are most likely cumulus clouds. Knowing that, how high up would you say these clouds are located?

Learning About Temperature

When people talk about the weather, the outside temperature is usually the first thing they want to discuss. Perhaps this is because the temperature is something that is constantly changing.

STEM Fast Fact!

Let's take a look at some temperatures:

103°
65°
-12°

The little "°" to the right of each of the numbers stands for degrees.

In the United States, the Fahrenheit temperature scale is used. Other parts of the world use the Celsius scale of temperature.

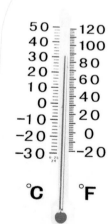

A thermometer like this one, which has both a Fahrenheit and Celsius scale, can be a big help when learning how to convert from one scale to the other. The circular gauge is for measuring humidity.

When reading temperatures, you could also say that the temperature is:

103 degrees Fahrenheit

65 degrees Fahrenheit

-12 degrees Fahrenheit

In America, it's assumed that the degrees being referred to are Fahrenheit. That is why people usually drop the term Fahrenheit and simply say degrees:

103 degrees

65 degrees

-12 degrees

Some temperatures have a "–" symbol in front of them. Does that symbol look familiar to you? It should, because it's a minus sign. The same symbol used in subtraction problems. The way you should read that temperature is minus 12 degrees.

Death Valley is known as the hottest place on Earth and driest place in North America. The world record highest air temperature of 134 degrees Fahrenheit (57 degrees Celsius) was recorded at Furnace Creek on July 10, 1913.

The freezing temperature and the boiling temperature are good reference points to keep in mind. You can use them to figure out what a current temperature means. Another reference number you can use is room temperature, the temperature most people feel comfortable with in their homes. Room temperature is 72 degrees Fahrenheit (22.2 degrees Celsius).

STEM Fast Fact!

Water is a key element in temperature scales. For instance, two key points of the Fahrenheit scale are the temperature at which water freezes, and the temperature at which water boils:

32°F = freezing point   **212°F = boiling point**

STEM in Action?

How many degrees are there between these two numbers? You can find out by subtracting:

212 - 32 = 180

There are 180° between the boiling and freezing points on the Fahrenheit temperature scale!

You can compare different temperatures to those of freezing point, boiling point, and room temperature.

STEM in Action ?

You can probably tell already that 103°F is a hot temperature. But how hot is it?

Compare it with room temperature by subtracting the smaller number from the larger one:

103 - 72 = 31

Wow. 103°F is 31 degrees above room temperature.

The lowest temperature ever recorded in Canada was -81 degrees Fahrenheit (-63 degrees Celsius). It was recorded at Snag in the Yukon territory on February 3, 1947.

STEM in Action?

How warm is 65°F. The easiest comparison you can make here is with room temperature. Again, just subtract the smaller number from the larger one:

$$72 - 65 = 7$$

So, 65°F is seven degrees lower than room temperature.

This temperature is comfortable, maybe even a little cool. Now for the last temperature, -12°F. The first thing to understand about this temperature is that it is below zero. That is why it is -12°F—because it is 12 degrees, or 12 degrees less than zero.

Obviously, this means that a temperature of minus 12 degrees is also below freezing (32°F). The question is, how many degrees below freezing is it? In order to find out, you'll have to use both subtraction and addition. First of all, subtract zero from 32:

$$32° - 0° = 32°$$

Next, add the number of degrees below zero the temperature is to 32:

$$32° + 12° = 44°$$

Now you know that a temperature of minus 12 degrees is 44 degrees below freezing. That's a cold day!

Learning About Climate

Although weather is constantly changing, there are certain patterns that the weather follows in specific locations. For instance, Florida is known as a generally hot, sunny location while North Dakota is known as a cold, snowy place.

What we're talking about here is climate, the type of weather usually experienced in a particular place over a long period of time. Climate is measured according to two conditions: temperature and **precipitation**.

STEM Fast Fact!

Gabriel Daniel Fahrenheit

A German physicist named Gabriel Daniel Fahrenheit developed the Fahrenheit scale in 1724. Fahrenheit was a creator of scientific instruments. He invented both the alcohol thermometer and the mercury thermometer. However, today many thermometers use alcohol.

Florida beach

Fargo, North Dakota

Temperature

Let's look at the temperature data collected at some prominent weather stations in the United States. This chart lists the places with some of the warmest temperatures.

City	State	Average Annual Temperature
Honolulu	Hawaii	76.975°F
Miami	Florida	75.7°F
Vero Beach	Florida	72.475°F
Tampa	Florida	71.95°F
Phoenix	Arizona	71.525°F
San Antonio	Texas	68.7°F
Houston	Texas	68.225°F
Tucson	Arizona	68.15°F
New Orleans	Louisiana	68.1°F
Austin	Texas	68.075°F

*Source: Infoplease.com - Climate of 100 Selected U.S. Cities

Look carefully at the top of the third column. It's labeled Average Annual Temperature. What does that mean?

Let's say that tomorrow you were going to Honolulu, Hawaii. Just because the Average Annual Temperature there is roughly 77 degrees Fahrenheit (25 degrees Celsius) doesn't mean that's what the temperature will be when you are there. It might be hotter, or it might be colder.

STEM in Action ?

How does your teacher calculate your grades? One of the most important factors are your test scores.

Let's say that, during a grading period, you took three tests, and your scores were:

79
94
82

Based on these scores, what would your final grade be?

You can find out by calculating the average of the test scores. First, add them up:

79 + 94 + 82 = 255

The next step is to divide the result (255) by the number of addends. Addends are the numbers you added together. In this case, there were three addends, 79, 94, and 82:

255 ÷ 3 = 85

The average of all your test scores is 85.

An average is a number that represents a group of numbers. Believe it or not, you already have a lot of experience with averages. Your grades are averages.

Every teacher has their own way of calculating grades. They have what they call a grading curve.

Average Annual Temperature is calculated in the same way. Temperatures are taken not only every day of the year, but at different times each day. However, you can narrow things down by looking at just four numbers. In this case, consider the temperatures in Honolulu for January, April, July, and October. You've probably noticed that these months roughly coincide with the four seasons: winter, spring, summer, and fall.

January	April	July	October
72.6 °F	75.7 °F	80.1 °F	79.5 °F

*Source: Infoplease.com - Climate of 100 Selected U.S. Cities

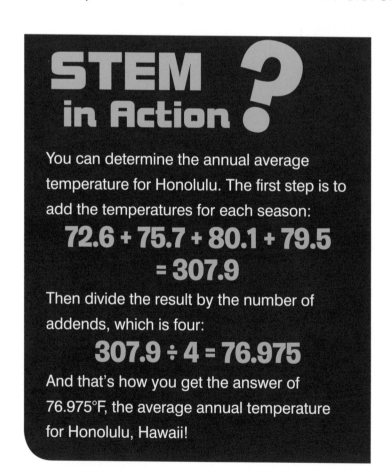

STEM in Action ?

You can determine the annual average temperature for Honolulu. The first step is to add the temperatures for each season:

$$72.6 + 75.7 + 80.1 + 79.5 = 307.9$$

Then divide the result by the number of addends, which is four:

$$307.9 \div 4 = 76.975$$

And that's how you get the answer of 76.975°F, the average annual temperature for Honolulu, Hawaii!

For comparison, take a look at some of the coldest average temperatures:

City	State	Average Annual Temperature
Burlington	Vermont	44.2°F
Helena	Montana	43.35°F
Bismarck	North Dakota	41.425°F
Fargo	North Dakota	40.825°F
Juneau	Alaska	39.6°F
Caribou	Maine	39.05°F
Duluth	Minnesota	38.55°F
Anchorage	Alaska	35.275°F
Mt. Washington	New Hampshire	26.675°F
Fairbanks	Alaska	26.025°F

*Source: Infoplease.com - Climate of 100 Selected U.S. Cities

STEM in Action?

What is the difference in temperature between the warmest and coldest cities. We already know the warmest city is Honolulu, Hawaii. But what is the coldest city? Fairbanks, Alaska is the coldest city. You can find out the difference in temperature by subtracting the smaller number from the larger one:

$$76.975 - 26.025 = 50.95$$

So, the difference between the average annual temperature for Honolulu and Fairbanks is of 50.95 degrees.

Fairbanks' climate is classified as subarctic with long, cold winters and short, warm summers in which much of the annual precipitation falls.

STEM in Action **?**

How does the temperature in Fairbanks, Alaska compare to freezing point? The temperature in Fairbanks is a decimal. Sometimes, when an exact number is not necessary, you can round a decimal number to its closest whole number, which is a number without any decimal places. Look at the Fairbanks number again:

26.025

Since the first number after the decimal place is zero, you can round this number down to 26. This makes the math you need to do much simpler:

32 - 26 = 6

On average, the temperature in Fairbanks, Alaska, is six degrees below freezing.

Precipitation

What's the nearest source of water to you at this very moment?

The kitchen sink? The pond in your backyard? The drinking fountain in the school hallway?

Did you know that there is water in the air around you? This is the same water that condenses to form clouds, and it can make you feel uncomfortable on a hot and humid summer day.

There are also times when the air is loaded with so much water that it actually falls out of the sky. This is called precipitation. The type of precipitation that most people are familiar with is rain.

For every minute of every day, 1 billion tons of rain falls on the Earth. Rain plays a key role in the cycle of returning water back to our Earth.

In an average year, at least 0.01 inches (0.25 millimeters) of precipitation falls on 150 days in Seattle, Washington. It is cloudy 201 days out of the year and partly cloudy 93 days.

Rain is a big factor in determining the climate of an area. The amount of rain a place gets can determine if that area is a **desert**, a **rain forest**, or somewhere in between.

What images come to mind when you hear the term desert? Sand? Snakes? Maybe a cactus?

Many deserts have these items, but what makes a place a desert is the amount of rainfall it receives. A desert is an area that receives no more than 10 inches (25.40 centimeters) of rainfall per year. And, although the temperatures in a desert are usually high during the day, they can get very cold at night.

There are even snowy deserts! The Arctic, for instance, might not look like your idea of a desert, but because it gets less than 10 inches (25.40 centimeters) of rainfall in an average year, it is considered to be a desert.

There are four large deserts in the United States, all of them located in the Southwest.

Great Basin Desert

Sonoran Desert

Mojave Desert

Chihuahuan Desert

On the other hand, a rain forest is pretty much what it sounds like: a thick forest that receives a great deal of rain. To qualify as a rain forest, an area must receive at least 100 inches (254 centimeters) of rainfall per year.

Mojave Desert

Kauai rain forest is said to be the wettest on Earth. The rain has carved deep valleys and canyons into the island, making it a spectacular sight.

Let's take a look at two charts based on data collected at weather stations in the United States.

Large Amounts of Rainfall

Location	State	Rainfall
Mt. Washington	New Hampshire	89.92 inches
Mobile	Alabama	64.64 inches
New Orleans	Louisiana	59.74 inches
Miami	Florida	57.55 inches
Baton Rouge	Louisiana	55.77 inches
Birmingham	Alabama	54.52 inches
Juneau	Alaska	53.15 inches
Jackson	Mississippi	52.82 inches
Jacksonville	Florida	52.76 inches
Charleston	South Carolina	51.59 inches

*Source: Infoplease.com - Climate of 100 Selected U.S. Cities

Low Amounts of Rainfall

Location	State	Rainfall
Tucson	Arizona	11.14 inches
Fairbanks	Alaska	10.37 inches
Roswell	New Mexico	9.70 inches
San Diego	California	8.12 inches
Albuquerque	New Mexico	8.12 inches
Grand Junction	Colorado	8.00 inches
El Paso	Texas	7.82 inches
Reno	Nevada	7.49 inches
Phoenix	Arizona	7.11 inches
Las Vegas	Nevada	4.19 inches

*Source: Infoplease.com - Climate of 100 Selected U.S. Cities

Some of the driest places are all located in the Southwest, or in the desert.

STEM in Action ?

How many more inches of rain does Mt. Washington, New Hampshire, receive compared to Las Vegas, Nevada?

All you have to do is subtract the smaller number from the bigger number:

$$89.92 - 4.19 = 85.73$$

So in an average year, Mt. Washington, New Hampshire, receives about 86 more inches of rain than Las Vegas, Nevada!

Las Vegas, Nevada

Mt. Washington, New Hampshire

STEM Fast Fact!

Dew

Strictly speaking, **dew** is not a form of precipitation. This is because precipitation involves falling. Both snow and rain fall from the sky. Dew, on the other hand, merely collects.

Dew usually forms at night when the temperature of the air cools. When this happens, the ability of the air to retain moisture lessens. As the water vapor in the air condenses, it ends up on leaves, cars, grass, or just about any stationary object. If the air is unusually cold, the dew will freeze and become frost.

Have you ever gone outside on a cool morning and found dew? What does that tell you about the weather the night before?

Learning About Snowfall

Have you ever been looking forward to a snow day only to be disappointed when it rained instead? Snow is a tricky thing. In order for it to snow, the temperature has to be just right.

Most precipitation actually starts as snow. That is because high up, in the troposphere, it is always cold.

As you learned before, the freezing temperature for water is 32 degrees Fahrenheit (0 degrees Celsius). If the outside temperature is much warmer than freezing, the precipitation that leaves the clouds as snow melts on the way down and hits the ground as rain.

Heavy snowfall can cause school to be cancelled. However, very specific atmospheric conditions need to be met in order for snow to occur.

Depending on where you live, you may have never seen snow. Let's take a look at some more charts to compare cities with large amounts of snowfall and those with little snowfall.

Cities with Large Amounts of Snowfall

Location	State	Snowfall
Mt. Washington	New Hampshire	246.8 inches
Caribou	Maine	113.3 inches
Juneau	Alaska	102.8 inches
Buffalo	New York	92.2 inches
Casper	Wyoming	80.5 inches
Burlington	Vermont	78.2 inches
Duluth	Minnesota	77.4 inches
Portland	Maine	72.4 inches
Grand Rapids	Michigan	72.4 inches
Anchorage	Alaska	69.2 inches

*Source: Infoplease.com - Climate of 100 Selected U.S. Cities

Cities with Low Amounts of Snowfall

Location	State	Snowfall
Houston	Texas	0.4 inches
San Antonio	Texas	0.4 inches
Mobile	Alabama	0.3 inches
Savannah	Georgia	0.3 inches
Montgomery	Alabama	0.3 inches
New Orleans	Louisiana	0.2 inches
Baton Rouge	Louisiana	0.1 inches
Sacramento	California	0.1 inches
Miami	Florida	0 inches
Honolulu	Hawaii	0 inches

*Source: Infoplease.com - Climate of 100 Selected U.S. Cities

STEM in Action

Let's compare two places in the continental United States. How about Buffalo, New York and Mobile, Alabama?

Buffalo   92.2

Mobile   0.3

In an average year, how many more inches of snow does Buffalo, New York receive than Mobile, Alabama?

$$92.2 - 0.3 = 91.9$$

So Buffalo, New York typically receives about 91.9 inches more snow in a year than Mobile, Alabama!

To put all that in perspective, calculate how many feet of snow that is. There are 12 inches in one foot. In order to figure out how many feet 91.9 inches is, you'll need to divide 91.9 by 12:

$$91.9 \div 12 = 7.65$$

So Buffalo, New York, gets about seven more feet of snow in a year than Mobile, Alabama! That sounds like a lot of shoveling!

Buffalo, New York

Mobile, Alabama

Learning About Wind

On occasion, you've probably had to consider different wind conditions. If you want to fly a kite, for instance, you have to wait for a good breeze. You may also have worn a windbreaker, which is a perfect jacket for keeping warm on a windy spring day. But did you know that there is a scale for measuring wind?

An anemometer is an instrument that measures wind speed and wind pressure.

The Beaufort Scale was developed in 1806 by Admiral Sir Francis Beaufort of the Royal Navy. It is the most common method of measurement for wind speeds.

Beaufort Scale

Force	Description	Wind speed (mph)	Conditions
0	Calm	0	Smoke rises vertically
1	Light air	1 to 3	Smoke drifts
2	Light breeze	4 to 7	Leaves rustle; vane moved by wind
3	Gentle Breeze	8 to 12	Leaves in constant motion; light flag extended
4	Moderate breeze	13 to 18	Raised dust and loose paper; small branches move
5	Fresh breeze	19 to 24	Small trees sway; crested wavelets on inland water
6	Strong breeze	25 to 31	Large branches in motion
7	Near gale	32 to 38	Whole trees in motion
8	Fresh gale	39 to 46	Breaks twigs off trees; impedes walking
9	Strong gale	47 to 54	Slight structural damage to buildings
10	Whole gale	55 to 63	Large branches broken; some trees uprooted
11	Violent storm	64 to 72	Large trees uprooted
12	Hurricane force	73+	Widespread damage occurs

As you can see, on the Beaufort Scale, winds are measured in terms of miles per hour. They are also categorized according to different strengths. The lightest wind, the one that travels at roughly 1 to 3 miles per hour (1.62 to 4.82 kilometers per hour), is a Force 1 wind. The next level up, a wind traveling at 4 to 7 miles per hour (6.44 to 11.27 kilometers per hour), is a Force 2 wind.

Using the Beaufort Scale, can you calculate the difference between a moderate breeze and a strong gale?

This is a bit tricky, because with the Beaufort Scale you're not dealing with single numbers. Instead, you're dealing with a series of numbers.

Simply put, a series is a sequence of numbers. Take a look at the Beaufort Scale measurement for a moderate breeze.

A moderate breeze is any wind traveling between 13 and 18 miles per hour (20.92 and 28.97 kilometers per hour).

In order to determine the difference in miles per hour between a moderate breeze and a strong gale, you need to find the **medians** of these series. The median is the middle number in a series of numbers.

A windsock is a conical textile tube designed to indicate wind direction and speed typically used at airports and chemical plants where there is risk of gaseous leakage.

Although they are not the same, finding the median of a series of numbers is very much like calculating an average. It is a two-step process using addition and division.

STEM in Action?

Find the median for a moderate breeze. To start, you add the numbers in the series:

$$13 + 14 + 15 + 16 + 17 + 18 = 93$$

Then, you divide the result by the number of addends:

$$93 \div 6 = 15.5$$

The median for a moderate breeze is 15.5!

Now calculate the median for a strong gale. If you refer to the Beaufort Scale, you can see that a strong gale is 47 to 54 miles per hour.

So, add the numbers in the series:

$$47 + 48 + 49 + 50 + 51 + 52 + 53 + 54 = 404$$

Then divide the result by the number of addends:

$$404 \div 8 = 50.5$$

The median for a strong gale is 50.5, and the median for a moderate breeze is 15.5. Now to calculate the difference, subtract the smaller number from the larger number:

$$50.5 - 15.5 = 35$$

The difference between a strong gale and a moderate breeze is about 35 miles per hour!

Learning About Storms

Just as water and precipitation play a big part in determining the climate of a particular area, wind plays a key role in providing storms with their power. The stronger the wind, the more powerful the storm.

Destroyed cars lie where Hurricane Katrina's 30-foot ocean surge left them, battered and scattered amid the wreckage.

The effects of Hurricane Sandy in New York in 2012 were severe, with flooding in parking lots, suburbs, and the New York City subway system.

The Beaufort Scale ends at 73+ miles per hour (117.5 + kilometers per hour). This is because winds stronger than 73 miles per hour (117.5 kilometers per hour) indicate a **hurricane**. A hurricane is a type of storm that forms over the ocean and occasionally travels over land. Satellite photos of hurricanes show that the storms travel in a swirling, circular pattern like water going down a drain.

Hurricane winds use another scale of measurement. They are measured by the Saffir-Simpson Scale. The category, or force, of a hurricane is used to estimate the potential damage a hurricane could cause.

Saffir-Simpson Scale

Category	Wind Speed
1	74 to 95 mph
2	96 to 110 mph
3	110 to 130 mph
4	131 to 155 mph
5	Greater than 155 mph

*Source: Homepage of the National Oceanic and Atmospheric Administration

With wind speeds reaching 175 mph, Hurricane Katrina was the costliest natural disaster as well as one of the five deadliest hurricanes in the history of the United States.

STEM in Action ?

How much more powerful is a category 4 hurricane compared to a category 2 hurricane? Take a look at the range for a category 4 hurricane:

131 to 155 mph

It would take a while to add up every single number between 131 and 155 like you did for the Beaufort scale. Instead, use a short cut. Add just the two end numbers and divide by two:

131 + 155 = 286
286 ÷ 2 = 143

The winds of a category 4 hurricane are roughly 143 miles per hour.

Now perform the same calculations for a category 2 hurricane:

96 + 110 = 206
206 ÷ 2 = 103

The winds of a category 2 hurricane are about 103 miles per hour.

So, how much more powerful are the winds of a category 4 hurricane compared to a category two hurricane? Just subtract.

143 - 103 = 40

The winds of a category 4 hurricane are about 40 miles per hour stronger than the winds of a category 2 hurricane. Winds that powerful could cause a lot of damage. You wouldn't even be able to stand up in winds that strong!

Tornadoes are another kind of windstorm. Like hurricanes, the winds of a tornado travel in a circular pattern. However, the winds of a tornado are tighter and more concentrated. So while hurricanes are not clearly visible on land, tornado funnels can be easily identified during a storm.

Fujita Scale

Level	Wind Speed
F0	40 to 72 mph
F1	73 to 112 mph
F2	113 to 157 mph
F3	158 to 206 mph
F4	207 to 260 mph
F5	261 to 318 mph

*Source: National Hurricane Center

STEM in Action?

Tornadoes are measured according to the Fujita Scale. Using the Fujita Scale, how much faster are the winds of a force 5 tornado compared to the winds of a force 1 tornado?

Use the same shortcut you employed earlier for determining the medians of these numbers:

$$\text{Level 1: } 73 + 112 = 185 \div 2 = 92.5$$
$$\text{Level 5: } 261 + 318 = 579 \div 2 = 289.5$$

Now subtract:

$$289.5 - 92.5 = 197$$

The winds of a force 5 tornado are about 197 miles per hour stronger than the winds of a force 1 tornado!

Each year, about a thousand tornadoes touch down in the United States, far more than any other country.

Because the high winds of a tornado are so close together, they can do tremendous damage.

STEM Fast Fact!

Blizzards

Have you ever lived through a blizzard? In many ways, a blizzard is a combination of a snowstorm and a hurricane.

However, the winds of a blizzard are significantly lower than that of a typical hurricane. In order to qualify as a blizzard, the storm winds must be gusting at speeds greater than 35 miles per hour. How much slower is that than the winds of a hurricane?

You can find out by subtracting:

$$74 - 35 = 39$$

The winds of a blizzard are roughly 39 miles per hour slower than those of a hurricane!

A severe blizzard has winds over 45 miles per hour (72 kilometers per hour), near zero visibility, and temperatures of 10 degrees Fahrenheit (−12 degrees Celcius) or lower.

Conclusion

Now that you have read this book, you know that math isn't just numbers on a piece of paper. It is a tool that you can use to understand the world you live in.

Math is how meteorologists know to tell us if we should bring an umbrella when we leave the house. It is how they know to tell us if we should avoid too much physical activity in dangerously hot weather. Using math to predict weather has helped people, and even saved lives.

If you have enjoyed learning how to use math to understand the weather, maybe you will want to learn more about meteorology.

Maybe you'll even consider becoming a meteorologist yourself!

Red Rock Canyon, Nevada

Glossary

condenses (kuhn-DENS-iz): turns from gas to liquid

desert (DEZ-urt): an area that receives no more than 10 inches (25.40 centimeters) of rainfall per year

dew (doo): A form of moisture that collects, rather than falls, on surfaces, usually caused by cooling temperatures at night

hurricane (HUR-i-kane): a kind of storm typified by swirling winds of more than 73 miles per hour (117.50 kilometers per hour)

medians (MEE-dee-uhns): the middle number in a series of numbers

meteorologist (mee-tee-uh-RAH-luh-jist): a scientist who studies the behavior of the atmosphere

precipitation (pri-sip-i-TAY-shuhn): a form of water that falls to the Earth's surface

rain forest (RAYN FOR-ist): an area that receives at least 100 inches (254 centimeters) of rainfall per year

tornadoes (tor-NAY-dohs): storms typified by swirling winds of more than 40 miles per hour (64.37 kilometers per hour)

troposphere (TRAH-puhs-feer): the lowest layer of gases in the Earth's atmosphere

vapor (VAY-pur): the gaseous form of a substance

INDEX

Metric System

There are a number of ways that the metric system applies to weather. First of all, when measuring temperature, most of the world does not use the Fahrenheit system. Instead, they rely on the Celsius Scale, which treats the freezing point of water as 0° and the boiling point as 100°.

Rainfall and snowfall, for example, are measured in the United States by inches, but these readings would be done in centimeters for most of the world.

Finally, you know that wind measurements in the United States are typically expressed in miles per hour. In the metric system, though, these would be in kilometers per hour (kph).

For practice, you could go through this book and convert some of the numbers to metric. Try it!

Converting Imperial to Metric			
Convert	To	Process	Example
inches (in)	millimeters (mm)	x 25.40	2in x 25.40 = 50.8mm
inches (in)	centimeters (cm)	x 2.54	2in x 2.54 = 5.08cm
feet (ft)	meters (m)	x 0.30	2ft x .30 = 0.6m
yards (yd)	meters (m)	x 0.91	2yd x .91 = 1.82m
miles (mi)	kilometers (km)	x 1.61	2mi x 1.61 = 3.22km
miles per hour (mph)	kilometers per hour (km/h)	x 1.61	2mph x 1.61 = 3.22km/h
ounces (oz)	grams (g)	x 28.35	2oz x 28.35 = 56.7g
pounds (lb)	kilograms (kg)	x 0.454	2lb x .454 = 0.908kg
tons (T)	metric ton (MT)	x 1.016	2T x 1.016 = 2.032
ounces (oz)	milliliters (ml)	x 29.57	2oz x 29.57 = 59.14ml
pint (pt)	liter (l)	x 0.55	2pt x .55 = 1.1l
quarts (qt)	liters (l)	x 0.95	2qt x .95 = 1.9l
gallons (gal)	liters (l)	x 3.785	2gal x 3.785 = 7.57
Fahrenheit (°F)	Celsius (°C)	– 32 ÷ 1.8	72°F – 32 = 40, 40 ÷ 1.8 = 22.2

Websites to Visit

theweatherchannelkids.com

eo.ucar.edu/webweather

urbanext.illinois.edu/kids

Show What You Know

1. Define precipitation.

2. Calculate the difference in snowfall between Casper, Wyoming and Grand Rapids, Michigan. Which city receives more snowfall? By how much?

3. How many inches of rain, on average, does a rain forest receive each year?

4. How many inches of rain, on average, does a desert receive each year?

5. If a blizzard was forecasted for your area, what could you do to prepare for it?